Multiverse

Mike Smith

Multiverse

Mike Smith

BlazeVOX [books]

Buffalo, New York

Multiverse by Michael Smith

Copyright © 2010

Published by BlazeVOX [books]

All rights reserved. No part of this book may be reproduced without the publisher's written permission, except for brief quotations in reviews.

Printed in the United States of America

Book design by Geoffrey Gatza

First Edition
ISBN: 9781935402718
Library of Congress Control Number 2009910027

BlazeVOX [books]
303 Bedford Ave
Buffalo, NY 14216
Editor@blazevox.org

publisher of weird little books

BlazeVOX [books]

blazevox.org

2   4   6   8   0   9   7   5   3   1

B				X

Acknowledgements

Grateful acknowledgment is made to the following anthologies and journals, on-line and in print, for first publishing these poems:

DIAGRAM: "7 False Starts on Living in the Old Neighborhood" and "From the Desk of William Carlos Williams: Notes toward a Speech in Three Parts"
Free Verse: "Clones"
Front Porch: "Anemone, Limpet, Mussel, Crab," "Opossum," and "Louse"
Fugue: "Mermaid," as an "entry" to the experiment "Aquaman"
Hotel Amerika: "Stevens at the Strip: Peak Season"
North American Review: "The Station: A Second Take"
Notre Dame Review: "Pound," "Poe," "Ahem, Requiem," "Rereading Stephen Crane," "Plan," "Frost," "Snake," "Giant Squid," and "The Woman Who Became a Turtle"
Samizdat: "Ode to Emily Dickinson"

The poems of section II also appear as Issue 30 of *Mudlark: Electronic Journal of Poetry and Poetics*.

"Ode to Emily Dickinson" also appears in *The Possibility of Language: 7 New Poets*, Samizdat Editions.

"Pound" also appears in *Best of the Notre Dame Review: The First Ten Years*, University of Notre Dame Press.

Contents

I.

Multiverse: A Bestiary 13

    Snake 15
    Anecdote of Defeat and Defeat 17
    A Little Song and Dance for the Honey Bee 19
    Hellbender 21
    Two for the Birds 23
    Zebra 25
    Dog 26
    Robops 27
    Opossum 29
    Cats 31
    The Woman Who Became a Turtle 33
    Anemone, Limpet, Mussel, Crab 35
    Giant Squid 36
    Mermaid 37
    Hippo 38
    Raccoons 40
    Fugue for the Fugu 41
    Virus 43
    Elephants 45
    'Hobbit' 46
    Louse 48
    Clones 50
    Manatee 53
    Ape 55

II.

Anagrams of America 57

    Predilections and Predicaments 59
    Plan 61
    Poe 63
    From the Desk of William Carlos Williams: 64
    Notes Toward a Speech in Three Parts 64
    Live Ink 66
    Pound 67
    Stevens at the Strip: Peak Season 71

The Station: A Second Take..72
Rereading Stephen Crane 74
Ahem, Requiem 75
7 False Starts on Living in the Old Neighborhood...76
Ode to Emily Dickinson...79
Folksong..81
Lessons..83
Snapshots 85
Frost..87

Notes to Multiverse..93

in memoriam

Emily Kathleen Arndt

To the Reader

The poems collected here are the products of an experiment into the possibilities of anagram as poetic form. The twenty-four poems of "Multiverse: A Bestiary" are all anagrams of one another. The letters of one poem have been rearranged to write each of the other poems. No letters have been added and no letters have been left out. The subject of each poem is a different animal, and my model for the sequence is the medieval bestiary—that repository of science, legend, and literature. I hoped to riff off the advances in biology and science that make up our current world and seem to show us just what a Petri dish of recipe and method life on this planet is—The operating principle of the anagram being something akin to the "letters" of DNA.

In the second sequence, "Anagrams of America," instead of anagramming a single set of letters many times over, I explored anagramming multiple texts of various lengths each a single time. Each of the sixteen poems is an anagram of a familiar work by a well-known American author. All of the letters of the source text have been used in the corresponding response poem. As in the first section, no letters have been added and no letters have been left out. My intention was to respond to previous works that, for one reason or another, have been important in my development as a reader and writer, but to do so in a way that would allow the works and their authors some say in the nature of my response; I wanted to allow the source texts to lie almost as palimpsest beneath my own work.

(One last note: Unless otherwise indicated, titles, epigraphs, section numbers, and section headings are not to be considered part of the anagram.)

January 1, 2009

Multiverse

I.

Multiverse: A Bestiary

Snake

The way a sentence passes
over lines (chased or chasing?),
I slip, sharp spoon in the sand,
trusting your eyes not to follow,
the forgotten first taste
of a forgotten world (it
was always bitter, so
it was always sweet),
bent on a return—like God,
but more patient, more mascot
than mastered slave, the fan
of every human monster.
Hosannah! I am the line
and the curve, your telescopic cock
and coiled womb, brash
survivor gone beneath ground
to ash and stone, spoiler
of upright walks on shady paths
hissing from the bushes (between
white houses that slide down to the seas)
a name you hear as your own.
In dreams, you want to wait
for the lit blocks to fall—those temples
built ages ago upon my shed skins—
to find I am there, the great
reminder, remainder, Jahveh's
oldest celebrity still freshly
performing, though I, endearingly,
refuse at times to give my best
show, ex-matinee idol
benighted by necessity.
Wherever any new attempt
to understand life extends,
I am there, ghostly as thought.
(Were you the one whose father
found me asleep and held me,

the diamond pattern spun
over his hand?) Your one story,
if I let you share it, stars me,
first word scribbled on the dark waters,
underwriter of the world.

Anecdote of Defeat and Defeat

Those afternoon visits to the West
Virginia countryside…Exhausting courses
of flies, flowers, and the feeble grasp

of weeds under a cow-belly sky
the wisest once deemed worthy of worship.
Blue mountains. Black earth.

Only this day, I ran to follow
(Was I eleven?) my mother, trespassing
her way over a patchwork pattern

of forest and yellow pastures, the ever-present
tipples and tracks, toward two stray dots,
unmoving, on the distant mountain

that became, in time, something laughably
incongruous: Free-standing porch swings
in a field, a chair and ottoman, no,

more sensibly, deer blind or outhouse,
the remnants of a rusty still,
some altar. (This should be the painting

of a photograph on the game-room wall.)
But the mother and young calf swung
their heads to stare my way. I paused to mark

the mother's warrior's helmet of a nose,
the bones easy under loose hides,
the lousy insects everywhere, swarming

over sores and soft parts—Trojans destined
to extend behind the ramparts, yet shiny
with surf. The wide-eyed calf stayed

beside his mother. Something like the taste
of hate rose in my throat. I guessed then
there would never be real fight in me,
but, also, that there would never be a need.

A Little Song and Dance for the Honey Bee

The jig is up. Your case
    appears so hopeless and
mysterious (How often
    do we look beneath our shoes?)
that it has been presented
    to Congress and the Vice
President shall be briefed.

    So many colonies
have been found lost that we
    noticed; there's been no word
on where they may have gone.
    In short, there's nothing to say.
The fact is that faith in you

    has fallen fast. We want
you to know we're grateful
    for your past service and maintain
that we wouldn't be where
    we are without it. And
we'll miss them, the arrivals

    and departures you taught us
as we came strolling
    over threshed and dwindling
grasses. What flashy flights
    from nowhere to nothingness!
As we have long admired
    that energy for order,

the selflessness and restraint,
    some attempted to make
your hives waxy models
    for our kind. The attempts failed.
And we think, reasonably,
    that the propensity

for regicide (Is it
    getting hot in here or is
it me?) can't stem from
    democratic impulses,
for we find hives seem to thrive best
    under less lax rulers.

That man, as a whole, must be
    considered responsible
for the tragedy may be
    beyond any doubt. Possibly,
you came too near our bent paths.
    Rightly, your work still melts
to nothing in our mouths.

Hellbender

Slide the blue river on a tube, cheat
with a shout the heads of stones, tunnel
the narrows, breathe in every pore
the constant spray

and stay

or branch off with a splash
to walk my fingers above the surface
of the water. God, it is good
to get drunk in the woods.

I used to jam together every word
that rose in my thought so long
as it retained a ripple of sense.
Here, I let senses go. And words.
Catch and release, since what we have
we are sure to lose anyway.

Let me loose my pants
for a dance
on this very stump, for the drunk mind
seems to get nearer these passages, these lit reds
and yellows, soft browns, and hard purples
and greens, so I let myself drop
to my fern bed. I sleep, calm, beneath trees
some early god made whose eye
now only envies as it kills.

From a distance.
With furious aforethought.

Which is why I refuse to return,
but turn,
instead, my bottle up
to this salamander supreme
I see swim so largely the stream,
whose only commandment
is to enter further the forest, mix up
on the way another batch
of the stream's bubbly, and imbibe
what you can.
                    I down it all
for the devil dog that exudes
this new truth, my patron saint
of having nothing to lose. I drink
to having nothing to lose. I rise. I drink.

Two for the Birds

1.

Poplar Island has no trees, so sea-birds
have no use for Poplar Island—barren

and dwindling on the mud-dimmed Potomac,
which threatens to send it under entirely,

tree-free, worn to a tenth of what it was
before. But some refuse to let it remain

this way forever. Thus, for a year now,
they've doused the sand with maximum amounts

of the sludge that slows the ferries and fishing boats
sea-gulls love to chase anywhere, even

to Poplar Island. But that's not all.
They're suturing last year's Christmas trees

onto driftwood to lure the birds near again—
egrets, herons, even eagles—who may decide,

one moment, to kick-start a new habitat
before the needles fly to ground.

Rootless and recovered Island
of the Castaway Christmas Trees, next found

beginning to blossom with birds.

2. Guilt as a Kept (But Gently) Bird

See it, the stillest eye that never sleeps!
A parting gift, yet one that keeps and keeps.

Whom are you running from? What must you owe?
Who draws you home from the places you go?

My neighborly neighbors sure think they know.
They don't notice that I notice, but I do.

Why just this common bird, he hardly peeps.
He is sharp as a starling, smart as a crow.

He has the funniest eye, it never sleeps,
and it follows me softly wherever I go.

Zebra

Reader, you're right to wonder who I am
to start this work again—tongue-tied, dumb-struck—
to shock my sullen self into movement
(because I won't endure for another moment
the way I have been) without the heart or breath,
the very letters to name these animals
or even the family of animals to which
they belong. But they are my subject and so
I will try to put in them my love and trust.

(All form is passing; persistence
is the coarsest path to glory; no one knows
another's griefs.)
                      Punda Milia—their name
in Swahili—these odd-toed, long-lived,
but busy slow breeders, as stunted
as any of the dusty grasses they eat.

And, sharing the scene, out at the edges,
with a foreman's indifference, a leopard
prowls the savannah, the relentless way
I used to eye from my bookstore register
a girl, the way I surf channels with my nights now,
or, rarely, browse stores for actual books,
roving, with worse odds, for delight.
                                  Fresh meat:
Parade of legs in no-nonsense stances of
(Must I say it?) a proper, middle-aged sexiness.
But she's sprung and has one now, furry head
lowered with her body, then shown pitched
under a tent-flap of hide, as the beast
I don't name—alive, perplexed—waits
for the teeth to touch on some vital spot.

Dog

The modern American obsesses over the human act of ongoing definition. As does the modern dog. This may be proven by a short visit to almost any suburban backyard. Notice these shallow holes, as if the surface has been, for eons, salted with meteorites large enough to survive the trip through our atmosphere. Eye these dusty paths skirting the dry limits of its world. We should say, *of what once constituted its world*, meaning the dull wires and gray wooden posts. These parameters now enclose another who completes its routes much faster than the previous tenant (who'd grown used to this way of life and forgot it had not been weaned here). Or maybe this new other now plots newer paths (jumping the tulips spaced carelessly as stars), anxiously away from the outer orbit, radii skewering the living heart of the yard. Maybe this other is not a dog at all. Maybe it strays upward toward that unknown yet no less definite boundary, only truly seen from the uppermost limb of the tallest tree.

O why can't we learn from these kindhearted animals and the endlessness of their endeavors? Even here, even now, the true task is gleaming brightly before us, if more demanding, if less exact!

Robops

Mechanical birds called Robops have been placed on rooftops around Liverpool to scare away pigeons, who are increasing in number and size due to a diet of fast-food.

Though the experts were divided, those
ancient adventurers brought jarringly
from their mammoth sleep beneath
the loose caps, thawed and serum-nourished

at a resort (patent pending) saw them
as reasonable and something, merely,
of a foreseen, not to say too natural,
progression. Of course, the pigeons

would by now be large and numerous
as babies. Yes, of course, the influx
might have to be dealt with, and with
a new method, were the human animal

to survive somehow. They dismissed
those claims from the street
that were sorry to report the falcon form
was as awkward as, say, a sestina,

and only slightly less effective.
"Gosh," they gushed. "They flap their wings,
they cry almost like birds, but they
can't fly like birds. Are there doubts

they will endure?" Inscribed on the talon
of every third one: To the eventual
inheritors of the planet: We lament
the possibilities for misunderstanding

inherent in many inventions. You must know
that these birds stood not as art
or idols to worship, but as mass products
of the sort of resourcefulness created

out of too great a need, a stop-gap
to keep what we knew we were losing forever
shiny and clean.
              "Oh my," they sang.
"We didn't really miss a thing!"

Opossum

I. Flick

Across the water and opposite
the renovated cabins lurks
the ancient lumberjack
the locals swear they've seen, working

simply to support his habit.
September's easy twang and strum
sets a sexy mood, feeding
a minor feast of innuendo

that leads to early swims in the nude.
As if to prove that the least of us
is past saving, the four-star guard
brought his brother, a nature lover

who knows better but discovers himself
admiring some rare specimen
away from the safety of the trail.
(Already a blond's gone missing.)

Yet must every chase end in this
slow-motion crawl, in which the hurt killer
tries to trim her lead, but the strange trees
he's been chopping are fated to fall,

leaving the starlet to rise
slowly to her feet and heave to town
alone? And is the story now said
and done or (Gasp!) still incomplete?

II. Prequel

They found him—funny, young—under
a gutter and soon grew to love him.
Suppose she cared for him first, lying

near his box until he got strong
and so aloof she saw it was time
to set him loose. Twenty days

went by before he returned. They swore
he would not remember her, but
she came out anyway.

He sniffed and ran to where she stood
and where she stayed until
they took him into deeper woods…

Cats

And now I will tell you everything I know about cats…

1.

They bite harder the nearer they are to death.
Ask my wise father, who waded in the wet road
to help this flopping stray that had its back
broken by our neighbor's Ford. The last time
I saw him in person, he still wouldn't take
my hand. But this was twenty years ago.

2.

An aunt I rarely saw
never saw anyone on her left
because she surprised one
and lost an eye.

3.

If one isn't eyeing you for sport, it sees you as food.

4.

The night before she took hers to be neutered, my wife's
college roommates rubbed its stomach until it came.

5.

Some exist long enough to turn soft,
some prove downright marvels, most
last longer than they should.

6.

Perhaps because proper cynicism suggests, in part,
sincerity, they fail to survive in Hollywood
and fare better in monasteries or schools.

7.

No scent wafts fresher than fear. More
than any other animal, ourselves excluded,
I've witnessed them suffer.

8.

Mother raised three sons but when the last
moved out, she was prepared and got herself
a cat. After it died, she got two more.
We warn that these things
sometimes get out of hand.

9.

Dr. Samuel Johnson allowed
his pampered favorite most anything.
Boswell, understanding, didn't.

The Woman Who Became a Turtle

Is it enough to merely survive? That morning
she left the town she knew for a hundred years
would have been like any other

had the day before not been her birthday.
There was lemonade she sipped to go
with a meal she wouldn't eat. Neighbors

and strangers gladhanded her, as our
mayor's speech waxed witty on courage
and obstinate pride. She let him slow the day.

As antidote, there woke in her mind
where she would rather be. She dreamt
of striped turtles in a pond. Fattened

by toxins and run-off, their algae-backs
mark them as older, even, than they are.
Heavy storms this time of year thrust them out,

comically, across the road
onto vast lawns. (A few drivers stop, stacking
these incidents against the almost

infinite moments of impatience.) But
soft rains only call them to the surface.
Slowly, obtusely, they come, scrambling over

one another, as blind as puppies, olive spots
jousting under the pale greens of the water.
(Yet isn't it easy to suppose God

is a turtle, wryly returning life
to its lower intervals of motions and rests?)
Was it enough the pond became wet

window, then mirror? Was it enough for her
to be only symbol, fussy shadow set off
from rushes or trees?
                          I guess it was not enough.

Anemone, Limpet, Mussel, Crab

Hermits! My daughter walks near you again,
forsaking my hand. This summer, we look
and step so carefully, out of fear
and love. She says the sea is kind
to reveal this run of beach between groins,
these trinkets thrown in tidal pools
we'd carry in a pail to show the others,
if we had one. She has regard
for the sea, regards it as a woman,
because she is human and she is frail
and free. We pity the funny mole crabs
that aren't shoveled into pails. We mourn
the little clams that stud the sand
or re-enter the sea, and frown at the riot
of the sporting birds, delighted
by architects and entrepreneurs
whose slow beauty is a byproduct
of inner growth and for whom growth
is tantamount to virtue. We prefer them
to those other unplanned works the waves
distribute, prefer them because we may
touch them and because they're testament
not elegy, elegy not objects of grief.
That the world is only almost
predictable must vex God, in whom
I believe today, now, this moment.
My daughter believes in God as she believes
in Death. She is young, so rarely sees
the moon in its glory, only that exiting
palimpsest of a moon in front of us.
She slips into sleep soundly now, so
doesn't start at our every snorted word.

Giant Squid

Postulate: Those ungentle mothers and fathers
fathomed the long nights
with hourly visions so large they feared
they'd open their eyes to some new element,
immersed in dreams almost bottomless
to survive the sopping sun. Thus,
they had to seem real. Now they are.

Definition: Colossal *hafgufa* or
twisted island or whirlpool
above that great, ghostly eye, harder
to catch than to kill, keeping to
Tennyson's abysmal deep (not yours, not mine),
surrounded by the food that,
like most every other creature under the sea,
it both eats and feeds, drawing down
an orbiting army of lesser lives
that feast on its excrement, a group
from which we mustn't be excluded,
since for a thousand years ambitious
Norwegian fishermen have been dared
to stray to spots where fish always bite,
propped up by kraken, that rarest fisher
of men, reasonably sure that moments
of real danger rarely come with the creature itself,
but in traps of whirlpool and wake
when it leaves the boats behind.

And it always leaves us behind.

If every story ends with possession,
just how much lower must we now
cast our nets, dredging another dream—
ancient, lighting its own way—
to the sloshing surface where it soon dies?

Mermaid

I. Internal Memo

Sir, of the advantages drawn from the ability of seemingly normal lungs to remove oxygen from water, we concluded the greatest has been manner of travel, though research has shown signs of only two trips of any substantial duration. One was her honeymoon, but we know they explored little of either place. At breakfast, she thought the weather was brighter than she'd wished it would be, and hinted that, by this, she felt grossly betrayed. Local reports do confirm this impression, but remember she was in love so most things written by her spanning this time we judged skeptically, then disregarded. We prefer the word 'ability' to 'power' because hers seems devoid of the sensual and, merely, an alternative enacted without the consciousness of manipulation or the energy for production in non-normative amounts. For what it's worth, she hasn't used her strength to personal advantage. We have yet to detect a pattern to her patterns. This troubles us.

II. From the File

Often, I mistake
boredom for safety.
Should you please me, I
should show this. If
I write, I should rely
on figure. Metaphor
is easy, not like
argument, as any
lover knows. You
descended, some storm
at sea, and then stayed,
easy as simile.

Hippo

The OB-GYN receptionist
swallows our sweet time not acknowledging

our presence, but we do not mind. It's about one
on Wednesday and we, as a rule, avoid

confrontations, unless we gauge we won't win.
We've both labored like her but without

the strong heart not to look up from that screen
at every guest's arrival. (It's a tiny office,

but phones are always ringing and they say
that they are ready to expand next summer.)

Is she in her element or does
she have to remember her resentment?

And what does she count on her two hands? I've made it
to twenty when she stands on her short arms

to retrieve our chart as if half her body sat
in layers of mud. Really, she moves nothing

like the tough hippos on T.V., but that's
the word I push below the surface

of my mind. She reminds me of my step-mother,
whom one time only I called a hippo

after she married my father. Or was it Tubby?
She did similar work. Sore eyes fluttering

hesitant as a surgery patient's, she'd rise,
get dressed, and go bag a Thermos on the table:

*Bolt of the car engine. Jolt of traffic.
The lid strays from the cup. The cup
slides along the dash, falls, rolls,
and kisses yesterday's.*

No life is easy. Not even a floating hippo's.
We sit and wait on our results.

Raccoons

Fans above start to hum as if even the house
now wants to be rid of its exhausting guests.
A door down, two young men yank their toy poodle
on its accustomed route, stand briefly by the sunny slope
to the trash site, then carry it away
before it rages for all it's worth at last night's scent.

The population thrives this year, despite
alligators (also thriving) and the worrying
rabies. Recently, at least one family
found themselves home in an enormous oak
whose twisted limbs jut over an open Dumpster,
and earlier this season some say a male, cornered,
maimed a terrier.
                      Years of weighty wisdom…

She fingers the week's worth of crumbs
left in her front pocket.
                      Tonight, she'll remain
on her bed until he's sleeping beside her, wait
as stars spread and the moon slides
over treetops, rest until the extra lot
beneath her window empties to only shapes
of shadow on shadow, listening
to the purchase of claws on bark, for the doughy thumps
as they descend to wet sand. Tonight,
one more time, she'll wonder what they must make
of the yellow beam, at showers of crusts bouncing
suddenly over the ledge, marveling
at the way they scamper after every bite of bread:
unhurried, unheeding, and unafraid.

Fugue for the Fugu

Not a matter of if, but when…

Some diver hears it at the table
from the very sister of his more
experienced friend—the time he had no option
but to gut a companion while wrestling
for his tank of air, leaving the man to leak
and swell there, blossom bouncing
from the underwater wall—as he tries
his first bite, which jolts him into some
nine year old self attempting to press
the nine-volt battery to his tongue
longer than anyone swore he would.

...

Fugu, because he isn't coming and
she isn't hungry anyway. Fugu, because
he adores the masterworks of those aged
last years, wants only the sculpted gifts
that arrive as the sculpted body
marbles over with its own resistance.
Because she is heir apparent and won't
evade the world's dismay. Or he types
rows and rows of code for median money.
Or she's never done any thing like she wished
and, man, he talks too much. Or, fugu,
since the fish followed her eyes
not her thumb's salty trail on the glass,
and matters were sure to improve.

...

Drink to the largest livers, weary sitters
at the table of the fat gods, to bodies
doused days in the rain that rise, reborn,
next to open plots, to old hunger
and empty dumpsters. May we pray easy
to ease us down our only way.

Virus

Are you alive? An easy answer
won't be forthcoming, since any answer
adds new meaning

to what it might be to live. (You're best
shown by metaphor and, even then,
the terms are upsettingly

terminal and not always reusable
after use. Still, I shall persist...)
You are the next last-known

castaways reeled in from their
disintegrating rafts—thirsty,
foreign, mysterious—

who bagged the mighty appetites
of the whole manifest of souls;
the deep-forest, deep-fissure,

deep-space invaders sent to be suffered,
but only on occasion, which stymied
the amateur sleuths

we had on board. (You're too proud to worry
exactness. Or is it common courtesy
to allow one's thin opponents

middle time to take the sad trip home
and set down their affairs in order?)
Relentless

as homemakers bodying forth
a host of brave soldiers (who, then, spider
through the sky without

waving goodbye) or the self-made
travelers given more miles than anyone
uses, will late research show

the truth of what went on behind the doors
you closed? When your arrangement grants
that the addled Emperor

is kept safe, in return his small sons
and daughters have been, traditionally,
subject, though not
the most fuckable of his wives.

Elephants

"And did you know," the woman sitting opposite me asked, "scientists now believe" (Our train would soon cross the border into Texas; it may've been hours since we last spoke.) "elephants figured out we kill them for the value of their tusks?" (She'd gotten on at Nashville, having parted from her husband, the trip attempted several times already. She wondered if, maybe, the ride was difficult for us both, and tended to grow more so as the day stormed toward its sorry end.) "Really. Someone noticed significant change to their death ceremony. While others begin forming shields for witnesses, a few elephants extract only the tusks to place them down in faraway grasses, leaving the rest to bleach in the sandy open. It doesn't help, but that's what they do. They now try to bury them in higher grass..."

(She'd felt our shoes touch on a turn and saw my groggy frown.)

"Then there's Jumbo, of course. He's famous. Do you remember him? A celebrity and, I hear, a wiser sort of showman until a lesser, sharper showman's people moved him to the States. Built as massive as a train engine, they say, but, unfortunately, only nearly as tough."

(Two softer elephants on a train, bent low on separate rides neither will ever forget.)

'Hobbit'

Pity that patient on the table who suffered
any number of operations
so we may reveal more of its unknown world.

Say, *Ebu Gogo*, Ever After (Wo)man of Flores
or Sumatra's wily *Orang Pendek*
who swipes your children
to teach her to cook. The type specimen
is a petite, chin-less grandmother; she ate
anything and was easily outwitted…

But of these phenomena, there
are many substitute bedtime stories—
Nails scratched until they bled
from where that splintered wood
entered. (Fittingly for her, they kept
growing for days beneath the skin!)

Someone says some words another
hears. Maybe she starts to serve
rose-hips and hibiscus by moonlight
and remains so strong she states
without flinching all she has done.
It is natural she suffers most.

Impassive Spider-women left
at the mercy of children and jittery
Mr. Mayors who gasp away
at their nutty beck and gall. Her hands
never heal, but later, they buy a house and,
it's said, outlive the revived heart of town.

(She even returns to school
at considerable expense, and vows,
with time, to trot out her own shingle.)

Ebu Gogo, self-aware woman
and little mother to extinguished
daughters and sons, forest ground-dweller
and limited user of tools…

Louse

Fly baby.
You will never fly.

The second smallest live thing
that this rubbed eye has seen…

Gossip-common. Cartoonish. Fresh dirt
torn from the not-news news: more
stranded motorists (shoe-eaters who survive
the sudden snowstorm) or early retirees—
the lottery winners, ex-machinists
and their furred wives shown trading all
for stacked maps, the Winnebago
and that char-less grill, wedded to their plan
of getting lost, of just BEING, since
it's always a hairy time to be alive.

Wintering, then summering, springing
and, last, falling (but not, never, flying),
an average scattershot small family—
happy mother and father whose kids
(padded, hammocked out of reach)
soon, so soon, stir…
                              And there's the dry season
that you do not flee, and there's the wet season
that you do not fear, harp of water, stream
of sea.
          Perplexing how you're still with us…

Resistant, persistent as an idea or the hope
of afterlife lobbed in the human heart,
we've trophied so many harder heads
that bore you.
                But to find you, we must
remember, when we see you, to pause,
to breathe, because, most times,
we've spotted something else.

Knowing your place, do you itch
to teach us ours?
                We know it already.
There's nothing beneath you like us.

Clones

                    1.

Out of an egg-cloud swirling, beneath
imagination's high, starry eye…

Because whether or not what we want most
is mastery or just not to be stopped
any wish means to want without end,

they saw themselves pass
through a Funhouse gallery of possibles,
exiles cast from a field of blood:

bent, thrummed, absurd. Sent somewhere
that waits beyond our knowledge,
they answered last into this late life.

2.

Penitent Masters…Mothers…
Rest here next to your lost ones, stone
eyes open, stone lips you miss:

Curiosity's sips whipped them out
of a frothing cup. The flesh of one flesh
has risen, was and is one, and will

be so again, shaped by your love,
reinvented, restored. Born, rapt
in your arms as if wondering at a story

they hadn't read, did they watch, then,
the record of that face, of bright laughter
scattering to silence in some warm room?

Did they chart the thumb's blue scar
and mark that particular stare,
worried over risks they did not embrace?

3.

Like us, grown strange and away
from even themselves, their lives
must have been something like death: life,
and a parody of life—not the one, not the one life.

They say something like love sent them
toward our sputtering world, and love,
we are sure, has no end.

Manatee

Between the shadows where my mind
has fled, in the gulf that had been
the promise of a better world—truer
and vast—in the scattered waters
of an armor-less, undeserved tomorrow,
there floats
          a whiskered thought,
the tattered vision of my torn self

(It is thee,
O Manatee),

twisting my body through my life.
You are God's apology and sworn
confession. Elected meat plopped
in that string of pools beneath me,
you sport the scares of an avoidable life-span.
You are the proven necessity of love,
all scars and essence, deceptively strong,
which sang to her, that July Sunday
at the tanks, a woman I knew, dipping
her hands in the water, while the trainers' smiles
were otherwise engaged, to rub the brown
snout. She would have tried to kiss you
had she any time though it was stressed
this might kill you. (She was pretty like that.)

It is, O brave and stubborn Manatee,
as if some strange Maximus started over
nearby, born, reborn, of nothing
but his sole self.
                  It is, Swollen and
                  Impossible Hump,

when I suffer myself enough to relax
that I dwell on you. And I do not care
to encounter what assortment of forms
might replace your secret order in our hearts
when it is deemed no longer necessary

that you stay.

Ape

I wonder if he's still at rest, still
hunched on his haunches somewhere
behind some scant Plexiglas view space,
the almost too-human silverback
that so consoled her
before I swore to do the job myself.

    (She was twenty-two and went
    to the soul-gray city to see
    she could swing it…)

*

In want of, not wanting, ways of being,
Sweet Beast (ruled at the end, as
I am, by boredom and despair),
I find myself (Take it!) in darkness,
awake in helpless prayer to you.

*

I hope it was earned and brief, the hurt
that sent her toward your small corner.

*

I remember enough of what you meant to her
to leave unsolved, as she did—so wise
to resist that pressure—the mystery
of her misery there. I remember enough
to fit most anything into this sketch
she left me of your life as long
as it preserves that twirled grass, warm
in your furry, grandfather's hands,
as long as it preserves your looks

of tortured endurance and defiant rest
(except that no one would underestimate
the sweep of your shoulders and arms
propped above that lynchpin belly),
and the magician's rabbit's triumph
of giving her only what she set out to see
that now means almost everything to me.

*

I've learned enough to want
to be good for that and nothing else.

II.

Anagrams of America

Predilections and Predicaments

Miss Moore, you ought
to be living at this hour.
Only last night, by way
of cameras, I rappeled again

the seven thousand feet
of an underwater volcano
(hidden with others
near California) three

thousand feet beneath the surface,
to see, jutting from the mountainsides,
these coral spire,
I insist, taller than trees.

(I still see that nameless creature
lie, nosing this thing
resembling stinging nettles
rising under a sheet.

A bottom-sitting fish
is pushing in sand, a shiny
fish is assisting,
and a wriggling squid

is gushing ink, eyeing
shell-encrusted soup cans, muddy
houses any crab
would gladly sign for.)

So discovery is but
the processes by which we learn
there is no limit
to what we do not see?

• The poem is an anagram of Marianne Moore's "What Are Years?"

Plan

> *Those who write of the art of poetry
> teach us that if we would write what may be worth
> the reading, we ought always, before we begin, to
> form a regular plan and design of our piece.*
> --Ben Franklin

1.

To be separate, anonymous, silent,
yet not without real power or pride, say
the tact and driven mindset of software
giants, ex-hackers bailed out by the F.B.I.

Troubleshooters, key specialists
flown in to exact purpose yet no
further ado, then flown back home again.
One of the sought-after, needed, few.

2.

Bound by boundlessness, appalled
by applause, overreaching
in despair—The poet at home
in a prose nation. He weathers his vast,
unforgiven country like a storm.

3.

By jolt, by dint of play, Rex Eternity
can milk every almanac list, render moot
our daily reinvention of the sky.
Many may act. More cry out. Unnerving Time

4.

exists for our misuse. In it: loved lover
and icy stream are lost. View
the damage done in Limit's civic name.

• The poem is an anagram of the four numbered sections of Benjamin Franklin's "Plan for Future Conduct," Labaree et al., eds., *The Papers of Benjamin Franklin, 40 vols.* (New Haven: Yale University Press, 1959-).

Poe

              ...And for a few dollars found
the Fordham undergrad (much more human
than most) to show me how you lived...

Then home to Baltimore, that nightly flash
of memory: the way closed-off vessels
burst like national cannon in the child's
white-hot throat.
              The Short History
of Modern Poetry begins, roundabout,
in an unnamed gutter, in missed hints
of a mammoth disorder, drink
for stiff drink. When the moment came, sham
politicians, lovers of money, just played
their low roles, then, vanishing, left
the body thinning, drowning
where it last fell off, vote after stolen vote.

This may make for the oddest story ever told.
An ocean from that death, my cousin,
your orphan demon swam into common view.

• The poem is an anagram of Edgar Allen Poe's "Alone."

**From the Desk of William Carlos Williams:
Notes Toward a Speech in Three Parts**

I.

Thrown from the chalky cliffs
of death: another birth,   and another,
everyone for the moment striving
and well, doing their jobs, or doing
nothing, stung deadpan, waiting,
plopped between one world and some stark
other, the dazed infant inching
up mother's belly, stuck
between that loved breast
and the softly spasming cord.

II.

Drops down, another dusk. Useless
the cloudless sky, the scant flight
of stars. Defeat after such dull
defeat. We are beset
by privilege and woe. We are
divided but no different.
Who will save us? Who will say
all's decided, that, at last,
all's decidedly swell?

III.

Beware the experiment found ingrowing
on the shelf. What is it but life
in want of greater means?
What is it but the crutch of self-love
searching for a wafer-thin faith?

Propped in a deadening appetite
of ease, I recall the quick comedy
of a demonstrating woman
(headstrong...underfoot)
caught by local news, surrounded
by a blue line of courtesy.
To the camera, that escorting cop:
"Your heroes all are dead.
Or should be."

• The poem is an anagram of W. C. Williams's "Spring and All," and "This Is Just to Say."

Live Ink

When I was seventeen, lean, and nothing,
you were nothing I'd ever seen.
All I knew of you then, I'd read
on a book cover's shrunken timeline: The Poet
under the gun, driven left and right, worn shrill
from the small press, betrayed by his sharp
poems: vivid...uneven...imprecise.
Well over a decade's passed since your work
put my white hand writing. Shall I now strive
to rush this unsure business down
on paper? Shall I risk leaving it
on soaked tables where it might be found?
Set down this: Living or dead, no one I've known
means more to me than all you then did.

• The poem, including the title, is an anagram of the body and title of Langston Hughes's "The Negro Speaks of Rivers."

Pound

> *But came to me then   a vision*
>
> *which I carried, though it pleased*
> *me not, this reef and wrack,*
> *resting place riding as it seized,*
> *sudden, upon my back.*
>
> *But came to me then and stayed:*
> *The poem as canvas, dried and rot,*
> *a worn-out, faded sailor's cot.*
> *Clearly I saw then   and was afraid.*

My father-in-law, Dr. Arndt,
met you once, not long before your release
in 58, while you held forth, pell-mell,
on the front lawns of St. Elizabeth's.
(Murray, not Walter, the butcher
of my beloved *Faust*.) Murray,
English professor and Salvatorian priest,
before he left a decade later
with that great American exodus, that
bold act which led, among other things,
to his granddaughter, Virginia, being born.
Virginia Marguerite, named
for two of her grandmothers.
In the Italian way. Virginia Marguerite.

He told me this on our way home from Parke
County, Amish Country, your country once
(before you shipped, were shipped out),
where we'd gone shopping for a chair
and to look around, had passed
on the road, seconds before,
two authentic horse drawn buggies
with Indiana plates.

(Behind us, the great
   golden sun dipping down,
   wine-red bubble
   under the back window blade.)

My favorite image of you
is in Rapallo, captured
opposite a middle-aged Robert Lowell
then included in Mariani's
uneven biography. A couple
of bona-fide reprobates, and you're thin,
thin as a rail, dressed neat in blacks and whites
and silver beard, but seem, for once,
almost at home in the world.

   (Bald farms,
                    and this roadside wreath.)

He was teaching Christ and Bible then
at Catholic. You were a field trip
for bored students and peers
who saw you, if they saw you
at all, as sworn shock-jock and traitor,
the one-time editor of Eliot, then
committed enemy of banks and Jews.

Ah, what you were in life, you're less
and less in death, but per
this enterprise, bedeviler,
what would you make? I confess,
I don't know what to make.

So this.

But then to set oneself (to be beset),
braced against the endless,
unquestioning present
and its all-embracing style? With this,

besotted with word-shadows, then the numb
clutch of madness (re: crutch), little thought
given to the suffering few
I hold dear, proceeding bankrupt, unheeded

and unheeding, poem after poem,
the poems like ciphers decoded,
then forwarded on in code? Is it dross,
this madness? Is it new? Is it mine?

   (It's been thirteen years since I first
   read you, 13 years but I still
   haven't read them all. For that,
   I weep, and am glad.)

And how should this obsession end, how
should it best be ended? With such hurried
speech, peppered with tricks
and the usual suspect questions?

With this pre-pressed image, a time-stripped
and faded glimpse, the stretched corner
of some abandoned untraveled world:

Up and well and shipped out, the crack(ed) mind
capped against swells and the chill wind,
ship's prow ahead, the mast behind?

   (But to have done this much
   instead of not doing…)

The pitch (past pitch) and the price:
The true returns are endless…

stress *truth*   stress *loss* (i.e. *the* loss)
which means Time. Venerandam,

then the catch…

. . .

Stellasue at *Rattle* sends
her succinct blessings. She writes
these "epigraphs are wonderful," but comments
she felt she could serve me best
if I sent her some of my own work

   (A man of no fortune and with a name to come…)

Rapallo, now there's somewhere
I'd like to sail to and see.

   • The poem is an anagram of Ezra Pound's first "Canto."

Stevens at the Strip: Peak Season

Water on the poster
rolls bluer than the sea, bluer
than the wide reek of sea,
grinding behind
a wooden dolphin's
endless arc.

(Pure burn: golden sun
disappearing like
a worn-out coin
in the cool water.)

The owner-operator
welcomes all indoors,
egging us on in song.
Others claim sky
is greener candy, that
candy is in the sky.

Now bloom of night
bleeds on the green water.
O we feel the free air
rising.

• The poem is an anagram of the body and title of Wallace Steven's "Disillusionment at Ten O'Clock."

The Station: A Second Take

He has three wiry boys and their pock-marked,
idiotic faces prove the oil
does get everywhere, no matter
how much gravel is tossed around.

The boys smoke, and too casually stab
their butts down to die in oily piles
of tires and bike rims, airy bits
of grime that arise in pockets

and roughly ring the station. Mom
is dead, but the middle boy is a rock,
has a tidy, gentle nature,
a grace that remains untouched

by his surroundings. Daily,
he waters the prim plant, which drips
on his dog's tail, and stacks quarts
of oil exactly as mom did.

The oldest, who will inherit
their poor company (if not
as quickly as he might like), has moved
to the big city. He plans to marry.

The youngest boy came too late
to feel strongly about the station,
but comics laid
on the big dim doily are his.

He stays, but wants to quit,
to fly away and into
a fiery-colored flag of some
other culture, not these icy grays,

morose blacks and whites, to fly away
before he no longer notices
the vivid rainbows that barely rise
to the brim of the day's oily puddles.

• The poem is an anagram of Elizabeth Bishop's "Filling Station."

Rereading Stephen Crane

Back home, and down, down
in the yard, in the fog, reading
yet not reading, I hear
this train head west, hot
and fast for I don't know where,
the dry whine fed only by the mood
of the sea, of the wind.

It hits me:
        America,
the miraculous, the absurd…

How is the eyed stranger met?
Any lesson learned and left off?

Once, those odd trademark capitals
lay like toy tracks slapped down
across a lost century.

• The poem is an anagram of Stephen Crane's "Forth went the candid man." The concluding stanza refers to Crane's insistence, to the point of withdrawing the book from publication, that *The Black Riders and Other Poems* be printed entirely in capital letters.

Ahem, Requiem

Granted, I've avoided this
all along. I admit, I do not
have it in me to scare up
another song.

Does it cohere? the poet asked
when he'd reached the end.

I haven't the heart to ask.

Wary, you warned you'd stomach
any pain so long
as it gave off the harsh light thrown
to fuel the shy poem's
hard way home.

Were there no regrets?

Poison, preached that pal
of yours, then mine. True,
though surely by then
you must've liked the taste.

(Scratch that.)

All the wracked and wounded world's
gone bad, a bully waiting
down a blind alley. When the blows
finally whistled near enough,
you sidestepped, and dared
no longer tarry.

• The poem is an anagram of John Berryman's "Dream Song #1."

7 False Starts on Living in the Old Neighborhood

I.

Wanda, our neighbor, out feuding again with Andy,
her neighbor. His apple trees stop the sun
from reaching her strawberry patch; her ivy's
inching toward his prize flowers. Andy keeps
a fine lawn, I can't argue the fact, for
I've seen him weed through a thunderstorm.
I've seen him drop a trapped squirrel, alive,
over the side of the pool he eases into
each afternoon, because he always said
he'd rather drown than burn.
                                I'd rather burn.

II.

How you tell apart those who own from those who rent
on Roosevelt: One, they're white,
                                with, Two,
fenced-in yards.

III.

Repetition, say, for instance, a scent
that drifts through once a day (meaning
discharge from a plant outside of town,
unseen and headed west with the river,
which is as fast a route as it is deep and near.
I hear that you can fish in it if you want.
If I were you, I'd try not to eat what I caught.)

IV.

…She found him on his side, his
open hand reaching for an unreachable hose…

V.

Gina, fleet of foot, passed once
around her house and school, caught
a light at Roosevelt and Sherman Avenue,
and so she stayed in her stride
until she reached Riverside Road,
then dropped with a pathway under the street
and welcomed the pale scent of river
seeping into her nose.

VI.

To date: paper airplanes and a wind-up race car,
a dustpan, a hat, and a muddy two-wheeled tricycle.

I hold on to all mine; Wanda throws her catches back.

VII.

So his apple trees keep the sun
from reaching her strawberry patch
and her ivy inches toward
his flowers. I'd kill him, I think,
but winter arrives here soon.
Plus there's a war on again. Each evening
at six, dropped bombs test the limits
of every sound-system on the block.

• The poem is an anagram of the body and title of W.H. Auden's "The Unknown Citizen."

Ode to Emily Dickinson

I.

I too run sick of silences, still language,
    the long take of shadow
seen on house, tree, and bush, sun's maze
    (heat, arc, dip, and age), eye yoked
to the tender ease of home.

Given: a poem is always confession,
      the mete end always both tease,

concession. (I am more
than this I bleed.)

Entered, the world is a jail (isn't it?)
    hooded, small. Beaten,

we burrow.

II.

Arrest of the heroic: to sap that hue
or thrust in sounds of the quick...

You strove to tell them
(but handed the moment, the world posed)

then hid and threw them fewer, your meteors,
dots tethered (my term,
my error) to the jutted edge of day.

(Ah, your glint I envy most...)

The wisdom is simple, but varied.
It's won
        by reaching down.

• The poem is an anagram of Emily Dickinson's poems # 241, 441, and 475.

Folksong

Everything is in order
and the phone's been shut off.
The dry engine turned over
with a dry chuckle and cough.

Each key's found a lock
and pocket, and I mapped
the exact route. I'll quarter lemons,
each sandwich I wrapped.

Toss your army bag over the seat,
I'll fill you in on the way.
Nothing remains for us here,
but you plead to stay.

If a capable dial reads zero,
all the tires spin and spin.
That the mimic miles stop winding
shall alone tell us we're done.

We're done and we are done for
but we haven't been far,
and all will be much worse
if you step free from the door.

So roll up the car's windows
and stay there buckled tight;
I'll scan for a good station
to sing us good night.

Fall asleep on my shoulder;
I'll rest my head on your arm.
Tell the children you love them
or just stare out at a star.

(For Limit relaxes as reach fails.
And after the day has fled,
a pall of fear affirms the hedged rabbit
is lapped by a charmed pride.)

O you see the hard trip is finished,
though can't accept why
the rash wheels each keep spinning
if there is no place to be.

• The poem is an anagram of Walt Whitman's "O Captain, My Captain."

Lessons

Often, I shall revisit this raw error.
And, whereas, I can no longer
remember a name, for some reason
I can never quite forget the time
you once stepped—thinner, taller,
more than twice my age—over
the shorn hill's lilac shell,
seemingly without sound.

I must have been sixteen or so.
I see you slip nearer, onto
the church's fresh cement...

I had been hit up for money
by strangers there before, but I'd seen
your face. We'd met. I'd gathered in
all the stories of that brash final year:
Senior season, how you led the home team
through to their last championship, despite
the risks, the same bad arch, so there were
no clumsy attempts at chit-chat, no
requisite effort to grab rebounds, or false
flattery of my form, only chill from the rain
and the level focus of our need.

I recall I had some cash, but
for once I felt on that night.
I said we should play ball for it,
knowing you weren't all
you'd been, betting you might
be too desperate not to find out.

Goddammit if you didn't win,
if I didn't take back the money,
press you to play me for it again.

• The poem, including the title, is an anagram of the first and penultimate paragraphs of the first chapter of W.E.B. DuBois' *Souls of Black Folk*.

Snapshots

I. Manhattan

Still pulled between mother back home,   *On the toll road*
hard men, and a panoramic thirst,   *between Cleveland*
you arrive end-stopped,   *and the state line,*
all bluster, knack, and thrust, inking
your bald America, the vision
not quite level, not quite...

And so I bridge, out of time, the life,
the same token shots,
                          and watch
from the deck as you exit   *west not east,*
into a shallow window   *slowly the miles*
in the amniotic wall of the sea.   *fall away.*
Accounts differ as to whether you swam
for the tossed safety line, or were,
even at the end, just passing through.

II.

Here's to Pain, Happiness's hipper cousin,　　　　　　　　　　　　*I see only the*
the devout navigator of Heart's　　　　　　　　　　　　　　　　*unmanned farms*
meanest landscape, you
we felt with us when the hard slap of light
first marked our eyes.

Sincerest enemy, quick teacher, un-dear friend,
borne witness to all we feel and cannot do,　　　　　　　　　　　　　*and more*
the cost of all we know.　　　　　　　　　　　　　　　　*makeshift wreaths.*

• The poem is an anagram of Hart Crane's "Chaplinesque."

Frost

There are others along the way
that I dreaded more, but this soon proved hardest.
You soon proved hardest.
So after weeks of loss and of only
more or less loss, I'd had enough,
woke up and got out. Seeking beginnings,
I headed straight for the end.
I caught, one afternoon, a bus
bound for San Francisco, the house
of your birth. But before I'd been gone
even an hour, I found them,
hooked to, of all things,
a scratched Plexiglas ticket window,
blue bullets on a bright blue release,
fresh from the home office.

Surely, they were my way through to you,
your way around to me. Surely,
this was the net, open end
of the line. (Though you should know,
this is really all a part of the game.)

Back out of all this now…

Warning: A Potentially Violent
Individual is one
                          too much for us.

Who is sullen and highly argumentative

One year ago. A year here
nearly to the hushed, harsh day, and what?
Unreasonably critical and scornful of authority

I can't get through to them.
I can't get them to understand.

Indicates a heightened resentment for those

Editors and other poets, family, friends

who are perceived as more fortunate

Stellasue I mentioned before, then
at *AGNI*, kindly Sven, who said
he was hooked, though something kept
him hesitant. Roundabout Eric at *CR*,
for whom a third time was not charmed,
who asked me to wait a year then try again.

> He'll write them all out a heady verse
> instead of a curse
> as these questions without reply
> keep fluttering by.

Voices persistent complaints
of personal misfortunes

Awakened somewhere
in god-forsaken Illinois, I undertook
a rough apology, an uneasy draft.

Shows unusual impulsiveness,

~~Recently, it has been argued…~~
~~The unknown contemporary shall…~~
Increasingly I began to feel as though…

becoming confused, loud

late works of this kind were wholly inevitable…

and easily frustrated

I found myself…

pacing up and down the center aisle

there, pacing up and down the yellow aisle.

(O, to be greater
than the sum
of your detractors, to be, yourself,
too lofty and original to rage.)

I tore the thing to shreds.

Communicates a verbal or a written threat

Other poets! If only
there were a spell-book
to ward off the worst:

       Several canceled checks marked "entry fee."
       A book of stamps, a heal-all, some old gin.
       A dog-eared copy of Faust, yellowed
       with a highlighter, and then

       choose an early chapbook from the bottom shelf.
       Salt liberally, and through and through,
       with bitter, histrionic tears.
       Shake well, then let it steep. Ah, let it stew.

Note: As these are only some
of the major characteristics, please
be alert to the show
of any unusual behavior

This marks the end of the line.
This makes sixteen.

• The poem is an anagram of Robert Frost's "Directive." The italicized lines, also part of the anagram, are taken from a notice posted outside the Greyhound bus depot in South Bend, Indiana.

Notes to Multiverse: A Bestiary

Hobbit—'Hobbit' is the nickname given to Homo Floresiensis, perhaps a newly discovered extinct species of hominid whose skeletal remains have been found on the Indonesian Island of Flores and dated to 12,000 years ago. Other terms in the poem are drawn from Indonesian folklore.

Elephants—After being purchased by P.T. Barnum in 1882, Jumbo was struck and killed by a train in Canada.

Mike Smith lives in Raleigh, North Carolina with his young daughter and son. A graduate of UNC-Greensboro, Hollins College, and the University of Notre Dame, he has published poetry in magazines such as *Free Verse*, *Hotel Amerika*, *The Iowa Review*, *The Notre Dame Review*, and *Salt*. His first full-length collection, *How to Make a Mummy*, was published in 2008.